PINKY AND THUNDER
ROYAL RHINOS OF AFRICA

Written by Richard M. Beloit   Illustrated by L. K. Benfer

For information address:
Crested Crane Publishing
22543 Madonna Way, Suite 100
Palo Cedro, CA 96073

Printed and bound in United States of America
ISBN: 978-0-9863851-0-0

Pinky decides on a plan of action.
He gets up early every morning
and scampers out of the bushes
and starts eating on all the lush
grass, leaves and twigs before
anyone sees him.

  He is determined to grow!

Pinky grows and grows but, no matter how much
he eats, he does not grow as big as Thunder.
He barely tips the scale at 3,000 pounds.
And, he is still rather pink!

The elders all agree, what a good protector Pinky will be with his new special talent.

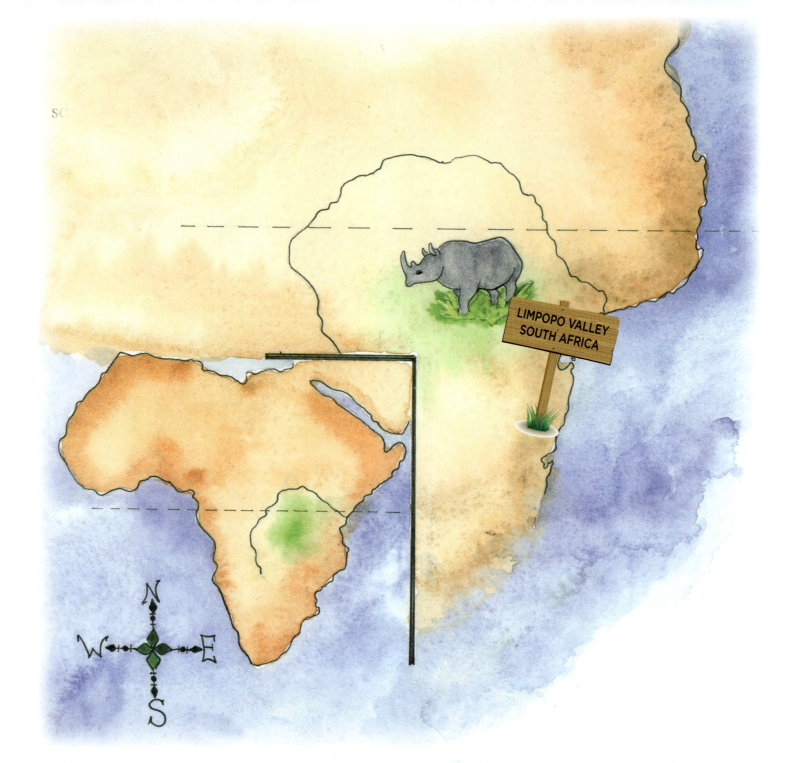

LIMPOPO VALLEY
SOUTH AFRICA